ATLANTIC EDITIONS draw from *The Atlantic*'s rich literary history and robust coverage of the driving cultural and political forces of today. Each book features long-form journalism by *Atlantic* writers devoted to a single topic, focusing on contemporary articles or classic storytelling from the magazine's 165-year archive.

ON BTS

Pop Music, Fandom, Sincerity

LENIKA CRUZ

zando

NEW YORK

Zando
zandoprojects.com

First Edition: January 2023

Text and cover design by Oliver Munday

The publisher does not have control over and is not responsible
for author or other third-party websites (or their content).

Library of Congress Control Number: 2022939789

978-1-63893-064-8 (Paperback)
978-1-63893-065-5 (ebook)

10 9 8 7 6 5 4 3 2 1
Manufactured in the United States of America

CONTENTS

INTRODUCTION

———

COME WITH ME, FOR A moment, back to 2014. We are in a crowded dormitory in Seoul, specifically in a tiny kitchen, where two tall young men are discussing the proper way to chop onions. "Don't mince it," says Jin, the oldest member of a fairly new Korean idol group called Bangtan Sonyeondan, or BTS. He's standing shoulder-to-shoulder with RM, the team's leader, patiently explaining that they need large chunks to make webfoot octopus and pork belly. Looking dazed, his mind perhaps on all the songs he's been writing, RM proceeds to slice the onions in a manner that makes you want to grab the knife from him. The duo trade jokes and share an easy warmth as they prepare dinner for their first-anniversary celebration as a group.

The other five members of BTS are elsewhere doing their part for the festivities. J-Hope, V, and Jungkook are cleaning the living room, stowing piles of clothes, toys, and cardboard boxes out of sight; they pause only to tease each other or show something funny to the camera. Suga and Jimin are doing their best to decorate a cake with canned whip cream, which melts unattractively over the vanilla sponge, forcing them to start over. In this video, every member looks fresh-faced. Baggy T-shirts and jerseys hang awkwardly on their lanky frames; they constantly brush their swooshy haircuts out of their eyes or else hide them under caps flipped backward. They don't especially look like guys who have an inkling of the career that awaits them. No—RM, Jin, Suga, J-Hope, Jimin, V, and Jungkook simply seem thrilled that they've been making music and performing as a team for a whole year. That they're still together.

I love this video because it captures BTS under the humblest of circumstances, before they became the biggest band in the world. Yet if you watch interviews and clips of them today—after tens of millions of albums sold, dozens of stadium concerts performed, two Grammy nominations secured, innumerable "firsts" achieved—that same sincere and unaffected energy persists. This aura, along with the group's genre-blurring music and stellar live shows, led me to become a fan back in the spring of 2019, a decision that changed my life both personally and professionally. My colleagues at *The Atlantic* witnessed my headlong plunge into the universe of BTS, despite me not speaking Korean and not being the biggest listener of pop. When they realized my appreciation wasn't just a phase—my cubicle decor and nonstop song recommendations must've tipped them off—they suggested I write about my experience of becoming a fan. I'll admit, I hesitated. Part of me worried about seeming like an outsider parachuting into a close community; knowing how passionate and protective the fandom, known as ARMY, is about BTS, I feared tripping some invisible wire or accidentally getting a crucial fact wrong. But more importantly, I didn't know if I'd be able to put the swirl of feelings and thoughts into words in a way that felt satisfying and true. I'm so glad I tried anyway.

My goal was to write a story that could be appreciated by someone who had no idea who BTS was. Nothing could've prepared me for the outpouring of responses that I received in the days and weeks following the publication of "I Wasn't a Fan of BTS. And Then I Was." On Twitter, my post about the story went viral. I received dozens of reader emails from fans of all ages (the youngest was a high school junior, the oldest was in her 70s and had been at *The Ed Sullivan Show* when the Beatles performed in 1964) and from all around the world (the Philippines; Brazil; India; the Scottish Highlands; Columbia, Missouri). Many said they had cried reading my piece because it made them feel understood, so they sent the story to partners or siblings who were confused about their love of BTS. Some told me that BTS's music had helped them with their mental health, personal losses, and major life changes. Nearly everyone told me my story could've easily been their own.

I've been fortunate to have editors at *The Atlantic* who've encouraged me to write about BTS. At first, I grappled with the idea of being an ardent fan and a journalist, having long believed in the usefulness of critical distance when evaluating cultural works. How could readers trust me to be fair and objective, when I was so open about my love of the group? But the more articles I read about BTS in American media, the more I realized the unexpected value of the fan perspective. First, I simply knew more—*way* more—about the group than most generalist writers and music critics; grasping the broader context of their work, their ascendancy, and their audience meant I could offer more informed analysis. Second, I possessed a basic level of respect for and curiosity about my subject that many writers lacked. Time and again I saw writers mistake their own unexamined assumptions or misapprehensions for objectivity. As a result, their stories betrayed an

A

ignorance of Korean language and culture, thinly veiled xenophobia, and utter disinterest in the group's actual music and lyrics.

To cover BTS seriously over time is to engage with many complex issues and phenomena—fandom, authenticity, social media, and taste, as well as artistic ownership, South Korean society, mainstream music's institutional biases, tensions between commercialism and creativity, and so much more. I cannot blame anyone for being intimidated by all of this. But I've found that the most interesting insights tend to arise from treating BTS with specificity—that is, from looking at the group in terms of its own origins, trajectory, artistic development, and relationship with fans, rather than largely viewing it through the lenses of the K-pop industry, boy bands, general fandom culture, and South Korean soft power. Some writers, in their eagerness to connect BTS to bigger trends and themes, end up looking past the fascinating and unprecedented story right in front of them.

As a journalist, I've seen a small part of that story story unfold in person. In early 2020, I attended the Grammy Awards in Los Angeles, where BTS performed at the ceremony for the first time—they joined Lil Nas X onstage for a medley of "Old Town Road" after RM released a remix titled "Seoul Town Road." Less than two months later, the coronavirus pandemic shut down life across the US and much of the world, forcing BTS to make do with sharing their music and connecting with their audience virtually—for nearly two years. Millions of new fans later, I saw them give their first pandemic-era live performance at the American Music Awards in November 2021, a triumphant return. Most recently, in May 2022, I stood in a jam-packed White House briefing room, along with more than 100 other journalists, as the seven members addressed the press ahead of a conversation with President Joe Biden about anti-Asian hate crimes and Asian inclusion. Among the attendees were media outlets from South Korea; as BTS moved to leave the room, one photographer yelled, the emotion palpable in his voice, "BTS 화이팅!" and "감사합니다!" *BTS, fighting—good luck!* And: *Thank you.* From a tiny dormitory to the Grammys to the White House—quite an arc.

This book, a collection of the first six stories I've written for *The Atlantic* about BTS, is meant to be a snapshot of a particular moment in the group's career: the period from early 2019 until the middle of 2022. These newly expanded essays describe what it has been like to witness the group's rise as a fan and as a culture journalist in the US and aren't definitive or comprehensive by any means. When I first agreed to do this collection, I had no idea of the news that was to come. Days after releasing a three-disc anthology album called *Proof*—which included new songs, old title tracks, demos, and unreleased recordings—BTS marked their ninth anniversary by releasing another birthday-dinner video, only in this one, the members announced that they'd be taking a break from releasing music as a group in order to spend more time on solo projects.

In the emotional and brutally candid video, they described how the rigorous work schedule they'd been keeping since their debut had left them exhausted and with little creative energy to pour back into their music in recent years. "We need to calm down. We've been racing forward," Suga said. At one point, RM shared his fears that taking a step back would mean disappointing their listeners. "But I think most of our fans wouldn't think like that. Because they know our sincerity," V replied. Most of the video went like this— each member taking turns sharing his thoughts and worries, with others chiming in for gentle yet emphatic reassurance and support. They talked about how pursuing their own interests for a time—a period they called "Chapter 2"—would be integral to their longevity as a group. "I think we should spend some time apart to learn how to be one again. So I hope you don't see this as a negative thing and see that it's a healthy plan," J-Hope said. Repeatedly, they emphasized that they weren't breaking up—despite how some media outlets misinterpreted the announcement.

BTS shared that this hiatus of sorts was originally planned to happen in 2020, after a final world tour. In other words, if the pandemic hadn't happened, many of the moments this book covers would never have happened. The delay also led to the group working two years longer than planned, deepening their burnout, but also giving them precious extra time with ARMY as a group of seven. While many fans reacted with sadness after learning about BTS's exhaustion and fears of letting their supporters down, most expressed excitement and pride—and the certainty that the group would one day come back to release some of their best work.

Proof is a reminder of just how high the bar will be. The anthology album felt like a fitting way to close out BTS's first chapter: a sprawling and dynamic artistic declaration for a group whose music is often overlooked in favor of their popularity, instead of being recognized as the very reason for it. I'd like to think of this book,

A

too, as a celebration of and farewell to an unprecedented Chapter 1. This moment may be the end of an era, but I believe the story of Bangtan is far from over.

LENIKA CRUZ

June 2022

I WASN'T A FAN OF BTS. AND THEN I WAS.

July 2019

I WAS ALREADY YAWNING WHEN I sat down to watch *Saturday Night Live* one evening this past April. The host that night was Emma Stone, and the musical guest was BTS. I knew little about the seven-member South Korean group—even though they had millions of fans worldwide, released multiple *Billboard* 200 chart-toppers, and recently delivered a speech at the United Nations. On Twitter, I saw plenty of enthusiasm from fans, but also broad mockery directed at BTS and their followers. While I knew they would be the first K-pop act to perform on *SNL*, I had never listened to one of their songs before Stone introduced the first musical break. "Ladies and gentlemen," she said. "BTS."

The *oh whoa ooh whoa* backing vocals floated in, and a teasing bass line began as the lights went up to reveal seven figures—their backs to the camera—in dark suits, an array of hair colors, and dad sneakers. They swayed from side to side, shimmying their shoulders slowly, and spun around. Then the one with the pink hair lifted his mic and started singing.

If you want, you can watch the video of BTS performing their breezy pop confection "Boy With Luv" on YouTube, where it has 21 million views, making it by far the most popular musical appearance *SNL* has uploaded to date. You might love it; it might not be your thing. Or it might not be your thing but something about BTS intrigues you anyway, like their synchronicity, their good looks, or the fact that they dance hard while singing and rapping live. Or how when the song ends, the guys stretch their hands toward the crowd, beaming and bowing as cheers drown out their thank-yous.

Before that night, I wasn't a fan of BTS, if only from lack of conscious exposure. After seeing them perform "Boy With Luv" and their 2018 banger "Mic Drop" on *Saturday Night Live*, I figured I'd at least learn their stage names. One week later, I could tell you that and so much more.

Like the fact that BTS's leader is 24-year-old RM, who taught himself to speak English by watching *Friends*. Or that he got his start as an underground rapper known for his lyrical dexterity and was the first member to join the group back in 2010. He was soon followed by Suga, a fellow underground rapper with dreams of becoming a composer and producer, and J-Hope, a highly respected street dancer who seemed able to turn his bones into rubber at will. I could tell you that the trio was meant to be the start of a hip-hop group before the company Big Hit Entertainment changed directions and decided to make BTS more of a traditional idol group. Then joined Jin, who originally wanted to be an actor but proved himself to be a powerhouse singer; Jungkook, whose prodigious talents as a performer obscured the fact that he was the youngest; V, who only showed up to the audition to support his friend and turned out to be a vocalist with an utterly distinctive baritone; and Jimin, the pink-haired one from *SNL*, an elegant, trained contemporary dancer who joined less than a year before BTS debuted in 2013. All seven, I discovered, do some mix of singing, dancing, rapping, producing, and songwriting.

After learning their stage names and origin stories, I absorbed their real names, birthdays, and personality quirks, as well as their musical strengths and weaknesses. Because the group's lyrics are mostly in Korean, I taught myself how to read Hangul so that I could sing along, albeit imperfectly, to much of their discography without the help of romanized lyrics. I binged their wildly entertaining weekly variety show, *Run BTS*, and watched random live-streams filmed in hotel rooms and recording studios. I bought merch, and began collecting physical albums. A month after that *SNL* episode, I took the train to another state to watch BTS perform in a stadium with 55,000 people—something I wouldn't have done if my husband hadn't happily volunteered to accompany me. At the time I didn't know anyone else who liked BTS. But just a couple of weeks later, I bonded with a group of other new fans on Reddit and began talking to them online every single day. As an introvert, I was stunned at how easily I befriended these strangers, all because of BTS.

To confess these details is both cathartic and, given the stigma around fangirling, a little embarrassing. Yet my whirlwind evolution from a nonbeliever to an "ARMY"—as the septet's diverse and devoted fans are known—isn't a rare one. After exploding in global popularity in 2017, the group (also known as the Bangtan Boys or Bulletproof Boy Scouts) reached an even greater level of superstardom this year. In 2018, they embarked on a world tour and appeared on a slew of major US talk and awards shows. Their latest record, *Map of the Soul: Persona*, made them the first group to have three No. 1 albums in a single year since the Beatles. So it was fitting that when BTS appeared on *The Late Show* in May, they did so on the same stage where the Beatles made their American TV debut. The episode wisely emphasized this parallel: The members sported tailored suits and mop-tops, the host, Stephen Colbert, delivered an introduction that echoed Ed Sullivan's from 1964, and the performance was presented in black and white. You don't need to like BTS to appreciate the significance of seven young Asian men, who sing mostly in Korean, being compared to the most famous boy band of all time on US television.

All of which is to say that I'm not the only person who was captivated overnight by BTS; plenty of other recent converts have taken to social media to recount their own rapid transformation from novice to stan. For me, the journey into BTS's genre-bending oeuvre and their community of fans has produced a joy and intensity I never thought I'd experience as an adult listener. Many of my friends and family members initially expressed surprise, if not disbelief, at my new-found passion, in part because they knew I had never really listened to boy bands, not the Jonas Brothers or One Direction or the Backstreet Boys, not even as a teenager.

At times during those first months of going down the BTS rabbit hole, I felt like I was violating some sort of social boundary. I wondered whether my age, job, and married status meant I shouldn't enjoy the group as much as I did, or whether the snide comments and dismissive jokes about people like me held any truth. Fortunately, I learned early on that being a fan of BTS means becoming intimately familiar with the many prejudices and hierarchies of taste that casually belittle the thing you love—and then deciding that none of it has any real power over you.

IN THE BEGINNING, I treated BTS like a puzzle to be solved. I pored over YouTube comments for phrases and terms I didn't understand, as though I were an anthropologist conducting ethnographic research. *Why are people saying "I purple you"? What does it mean to have a "bias" or a "bias wrecker" or to be "OT7"? Why is Jungkook called the "golden maknae"? Why are people praising Jin as a "stable king" or teasing RM as "god of destruction"? Why should* sasaengs, *"solos," and "mantis" be avoided at all costs? What's tasty in Busan?* Inside jokes and neologisms abounded, and I spent long hours after work deciphering them. In my spare time, I delved into BTS's extensive discography, stumbling across neo-soul numbers, thundering ballads, savage rap cyphers, and undeniable pop gems. I watched not only music videos and performances, but also meme compilations, dance practices, interviews, and explanations of the complicated fictional universe running through BTS's work, in which members play alternate-world versions of themselves undergoing a painful coming of age. I tried to approach the group with a distance that came naturally to me as a journalist but that was also probably informed by an inchoate desire to not become a boy-band fan for the first time in my life, at age 28.

The more I watched, listened, and learned, though, the less I cared. I watched BTS perform their 2018 anthem "Idol" on *The Tonight Show* and wondered how their lungs didn't explode from exertion. I watched the sumptuous short film for their 2016 hit "Blood, Sweat & Tears" and couldn't tell whether I was more impressed by the mesmerizing choreography or the high-concept storytelling. And I was entranced by the video for "Spring Day," with its dreamlike cinematography and references to Ursula K. Le Guin's story "The Ones Who Walk Away from Omelas" and Bong Joon-ho's film *Snowpiercer*. When I learned that the song is often interpreted as a tribute to the school-age victims of 2014's Sewol ferry disaster, in which hundreds of teen-agers drowned, I replayed the video and cried. Perhaps because of my own narrow assumptions, I hadn't expected to find so much emotion and meaning in BTS's work. I felt as though I had stumbled upon a secret—except it was one that millions of other people already knew about and had been trying to share with the world for years. I had entered this world a skeptic, but a curious one, and I'd been won over.

BTS were by no means destined for such heights, having debuted with a tiny company in a K-pop industry ruled by three giant record labels. The group's outsider status, which limited their access to all-important promotional opportunities within Korean media, could have spelled doom; counterintuitively, it proved to be one of their greatest strengths. Since at least 2017, when BTS broke out on the global stage, critics have been trying to formulate a unified theory to explain their success in the mainstream US music scene in particular, eclipsing other K-pop crossovers in terms of album sales, concert attendance, and listenership. These writers invariably, and astutely, point to the group's early adoption and savvy use of social media. From their earliest days, members would post video diaries of themselves discussing their lives, talking about recording music or practicing for shows, and answering ARMY questions. They did so with a candor that was atypical for idol groups and established a profound connection with fans, who in turn helped them smash record after record. Critics also cite BTS's socially conscious lyrics, their openness about taboos such as mental health, their empathy for the struggles of younger generations, and

A

their emphatic message of self-love—all of which are powerful reasons, but which are secondary to the resonance of the actual music itself.

Complicating BTS's rise to popularity, of course, are the politics of any non-American group dominating the US charts. The South Korean music critic Kim Youngdae told me that when he attended BTS's first American performance in 2014 in Los Angeles, a crowd of a couple hundred people seemed huge to him. In 2017, he attended the Billboard Music Awards, where BTS shocked viewers by winning the Top Social Artist Award and breaking Justin Bieber's six-year streak. After the ceremony, bewildered American journalists in the audience asked Kim to explain who these guys were. Predictably, the win also led to racist backlash online from people scoffing at the "Asian One Direction."

Such knee-jerk reactions stem from a cultural tendency to see Asian musical performers—and non-English-speaking artists in general—as inferior, said Kim, who has published a book about BTS. "The American mainstream music industry is really hesitant to call Asian artists 'pop stars.' They're okay with characterizing them as a subculture, or as an Asian American movement," Kim told me. "But the entertainment industry always has to acknowledge the hottest or biggest thing, whether they like it or not." This institutional conservatism was precisely what the massive numbers of ARMYs were equipped to overcome, Kim said: By voting for BTS for Top Social Artist (an award the group has won three years in a row), buying their music, and streaming their videos, fans forced the industry to pay attention.

As a critic who has followed them from the start, Kim has his own explanation for BTS's crossover success. "I call them the most advanced and the most evolved K-pop idol group ever," he told me. "Because they got everything the K-pop industry already had, but they had more: authenticity, artistry, artistic freedom, more genuine close relationships with the audience, and a very consistent thematic progression [in their work]." His book, *BTS: The Review*, is a track-by-track analysis of the group's discography that traces their sonic evolution. One of his favorite songs is called "Fake Love," which he reads in part as a commentary on the anxieties of the artist-fan relationship: "I aim to erase myself to become your doll," goes one line, according to English translations by Jiye Kim, also known as Wisha. (Author's note: Kim has given me permission to use her translations throughout the rest of this book.)

With the group's international success has come a resistance based not so much on their talent or music, but on their identity as K-pop idols. For some, BTS's

Koreanness is reason enough to dismiss them, as one *Teen Vogue* piece argued after an Australian TV network ran a xenophobic segment about the group. (Individual members are also regularly subjected to racist online attacks.) It's common to see critics make rude comments about BTS because of their youth or their boy-band status. The author of a recent *New York Times* story said she wanted to "gag" after learning some people saw both Madonna and "a K-pop band of 20-somethings" as "legendary."

The tradition of sneering at "boy bands" and their fans—who are often, but not always, young women—transcends national borders and is an old one rooted in ageism and misogyny. While comparisons between BTS and the Beatles can sometimes be reductive, they are instructive in at least one way: When the English band's fanbase was considered mostly young and female, male music critics generally regarded the Beatles as unserious and commercially minded rather than artistic. The archetype of the teen-girl fan has long served to diminish young women, in turn denigrating the cultural works they embrace. Brodie Lancaster, in a 2015 *Pitchfork* piece, put it like this:

> When fame is girded by a swelling teenage, female fanbase immediately, that celebrity becomes false, temporary, and unearned. We're

always grappling for a reason to disregard the value of a popular—and populist—product because blindly embracing it means the market research and Simon Cowell-eque figures behind it have duped us again. The presence of teen girls offers up a handy barometer: if they like something you can be rest assured it's not worth a serious listener's ear.

Still, no amount of scorn or denial can negate this demographic's cultural, or economic, power. When forced to acknowledge this reality, some critics adopt a vocabulary of coded condescension. In their telling, fans become "squealing," "rabid," "crazed," and other terms meant to pathologize certain modes of enjoyment as juvenile, animalistic, or dangerous. Sometimes this language is deployed without any ill intent at all, so inured have its users become to the meaning of their words.

While this stigma extends to BTS's supporters— even *SNL*'s promos played off the idea of ARMYs as mindless tween fangirls—Kim crucially believes the "boy band" label isn't entirely accurate to apply to the group. "When Americans see the handsome boys dancing together, for them that's obviously the format of the boy band," Kim said. But for Korean people and for fans, he added, BTS is "more like a hip-hop group with vocal abilities who can also dance supremely well . . .

For a lot of people, 'boy band' would automatically discount their musical ability and authenticity." Because the "boy band" label is so limiting, I tend to explain BTS's appeal like this: Imagine if the players on your favorite sports team (the members train like athletes, after all) were also your favorite musicians and the stars of your favorite reality-TV show and you also thought of them as family members.

When talking to people who are unfamiliar with BTS for the first time, I'm often taken aback by some of the questions I receive. *Is there any juicy drama? Do they get along with each other? Who is the best and who is the worst? Who's the Justin Timberlake of the group?* Instead of answering, I usually pause to explain the basics. Like the fact that BTS treats every member as equally essential to the group and equally deserving of support—a principle that ARMY takes seriously too. I add that most fans resist stereotyping individual members as, say, "The Bad Boy" or "The Face of the Band" or "The Sensitive One." This aversion to flattening perhaps makes it harder at first for newcomers to get a handle on what superficially distinguishes each member from one another. But those who eventually do realize how satisfying it is to follow a group of guys who seem comfortable with their imperfections, contradictions, and different personas.

Even so, ARMY is no monolith; this community comprises followers of all ages, races, genders, nationalities, and religious backgrounds. People are often surprised when I explain how much of the fandom is in their 30s and older, with full-time jobs and families. At concerts, you can find people holding signs spotlighting "Dads for BTS" and "Lesbians for Taehyung," or waving the flags of their home countries. While the community's ethos of inclusion is one of its strengths, ARMY's size also means that ugly elements do exist and internal disagreements can inevitably arise, as is the case with any fanbase. For example, last weekend it was announced that BTS would perform in Saudi Arabia in October. This prompted both elation from many Arab and Muslim fans in the region and criticism from others who pointed, in part, to the country's human-rights abuses and the fact that BTS has raised more than $2 million for UNICEF, which is providing aid for victims of the Saudi-fueled conflict in Yemen. Most new fans I've spoken with, however, describe ARMY as an unusually welcoming community that works to address bad behavior within its ranks. For example, it is common to see ARMYs on social media mobilizing and self-moderating around artist privacy, online harassment, misinformation, exclusionary language, gatekeeping, and general etiquette. ARMYs also regularly educate and critique one another on inter-fandom issues such as anti-blackness and cultural insensitivity or appropriation.

Like myself, the writer and editor Laura Hudson first encountered BTS through *SNL* and posted about her experience on Twitter. "I wrote that tweet, and then ARMY came. And I've had fandoms come for me online before," Hudson told me, noting her long history of covering events such as Comic-Con and E3, and shows like *Game of Thrones* and *The Walking Dead*. With ARMY, though, the response was "so uniformly positive." Despite being wary of positivity culture, Hudson was surprised by how encouraging and kind people were, recommending videos and offering advice. "People were like, yeah it's great, love it with us! That's what I wish more fandom was like," Hudson said. "As a journalist, there's the immediately skeptical part of me where I'm like, *Is it a cult?*" she went on. "But if it is a cult . . . it seems like one that's focused on positivity and acceptance."

As new and slightly older fans, we talked about not being able to have meaningful discussions about BTS with many people in our lives, and about how tiring it is to constantly, on some level, be policing our enjoyment. She told me about all the things she likes about BTS—their "nontraditional presentation of masculinity," the joyfulness of their performances, the dizzying complexity of their storytelling—and explained how, despite her tendency to approach most things with cynicism, the group "manages to get past my censors of, 'This is contrived,' or 'This is manipulative.'" Then Hudson sighed, noting how so many social forces get in the way of people allowing themselves to love what they love. "The simplest thing about it is: It makes me happy," Hudson told me of BTS's music. "But if it were also secretly garbage, I wouldn't be able to enjoy it."

During my initial tumble down the BTS rabbit hole, I noticed a pattern in the comments section for YouTube videos: preemptive disavowal followed by effusive praise. "Never heard of these guys, but that was some Michael Jackson–level stuff." "I've avoided them for years at this point, but I finally got sucked in. I get it now." "Don't like boy bands but these guys are athletes . . . respect." While I understood this impulse, I started to resent it. The group's music and performance chops speak for themselves and shouldn't require a caveat; the need to supply one says more about the speaker than it does about BTS.

While writing this piece, I thought a lot about the concept of *guilty pleasure*, a term that doesn't feel quite right for what BTS is to me. I don't feel guilty so much as I sometimes feel like I *should* feel guilty. Perhaps the biggest reason I don't feel guilty is because I do not fear, deep down, that the thing I like is actually bad and shallow. On the contrary, I believe BTS's music and the messages it contains are beautiful and deserve greater critical consideration than they have received thus far.

While tangling with some of these thoughts, I revisited a 2018 *New Yorker* piece in which the television critic Emily Nussbaum argued against calling the CW series *Jane the Virgin* a "guilty pleasure." I was struck by how much of her analysis of that show can also apply to BTS: "A bright-pink filibuster exposing the layers in what the world regards as shallow" could describe the EP *Map of the Soul: Persona*, which invokes Jungian psychology to continue BTS's exploration of identity. "A deeply heartfelt production . . . sophisticated about and truly interested in all the varieties of love, from familial to carnal" could refer to the ambitious *Love Yourself* trilogy, in particular songs such as "Outro: Her," "Serendipity," "Trivia: Love," "Epiphany," and "134340." Nussbaum also called *Jane the Virgin* "a smart show that parents and teen-agers can watch together—which, in a better world, might be a recommendation to a larger audience." Indeed, many BTS fans are parents or grandparents or young kids, but *great for the whole family* is a label that rarely conjures much respect, in part because it implies work that isn't challenging or distinctive. Further, some US audiences might have preconceived notions about the culturally specific formats of telenovela and K-pop, and as a result fail to evaluate *Jane the Virgin* and BTS on their own terms.

In short, it takes real effort to unlearn a lifetime's worth of social messaging about what kind of pop culture is okay to take seriously. For me and many others, it helped that BTS offered more than entertainment. Listening to their music and learning more about the members' personal struggles allowed me to better cope with an ongoing anxiety disorder and prompted me to take better care of my physical health. A few months before I discovered BTS, I had gone back on medication to help calm unrelenting agoraphobia-triggered panic attacks. At my worst, even walking a couple of blocks to the grocery store felt like an insurmountable task. Going to work every day was a struggle. Sometimes I couldn't bring myself to step on the train, and when I did I counted the seconds between stations, until the subway doors opened again. I had all but stopped getting dinner with friends, traveling to see family, going to the movies—because my fear controlled my life.

A

Though my recovery began before I discovered BTS, my still-new love of the group pushed me to test myself, to see if I was capable of doing things that made me happy, in defiance of my anxiety. I bought two train tickets for me and my partner from Washington, DC, to Newark, New Jersey, and two tickets to see BTS at MetLife Stadium. During our trip, the fear gnawed at the edges of my brain but was dulled by the thrill of being back out in the world again. For years, when my agoraphobia was at its worst, I had told myself that I was the kind of person who didn't do certain things— crowds, busy restaurants, spontaneous travel, road trips, happy hour, music festivals. I had learned to do without. But at MetLife, surrounded by thousands of strangers who did not feel like strangers, I started to rewrite that narrative. I could no longer think of a good enough reason to continue denying myself joy.

There were moments during the first month after that *SNL* episode aired when I leaned hard into my BTS fandom. It was almost as though beneath my excitement lay a fear that this hallucination I was sharing with millions of other people would evaporate. That I'd go back to being an adult who didn't follow a boy band as a hobby and who rolled her eyes at earnest lyrics about loving oneself. Obviously, that hasn't happened.

The magic remains and the hallucination continues, only as time passes it feels less like a dream and more like regular life. *I'll just learn their names*, I told myself back in April. Somewhere out there, seven guys named Namjoon, Seokjin, Yoongi, Hoseok, Jimin, Taehyung, and Jungkook were probably smiling at me.

A

BTS's "DYNAMITE" COULD UPEND THE MUSIC INDUSTRY

September 2020

WHEN A RECORD IS BROKEN, or a new one is set, it can say as much about the institution or industry in question as it does the talent of the winner. This is especially true in American entertainment. Halle Berry becoming the first (and only) Black woman to win a Best Actress Oscar, in 2002, was both an affirmation of her excellence *and* a testament to Hollywood's racist history. America Ferrera becoming the first Latina to win a Lead Actress Emmy was a celebration of her work *and* a reflection of TV's problems with representation. The corollary to an individual's historic win is often a system's historic failure.

On Monday, BTS became the first entirely South Korean act to have a No. 1 single on the *Billboard* Hot 100 with their new funk-inflected, disco-pop song "Dynamite"—the latest evidence of the group's superstardom. They've been everywhere this year. If you didn't see the septet ringing in 2020 with a confetti-filled concert in Times Square, you may have seen them onstage with Lil Nas X at the Grammys. You may have caught them joking with James Corden on "Carpool Karaoke," or when they shut down Grand Central Station for *The Tonight Show*, or when they performed while coiffed to the nines at Sunday's MTV Video Music Awards. (Or maybe you heard about BTS when they donated $1 million to Black Lives Matter this summer, around the time that K-pop fans were the subject of constant media attention for their political activism.)

Though BTS has sold out stadiums around the world and occasionally breaks Twitter, they didn't land the top spot on the Hot 100 until they released a song entirely in English. It's a huge feat for a group that debuted on a small record label seven years ago, underdogs even in their home country. Speaking to international press last night, the members talked about crying when they learned of the news, and how it made them think back to their humble and difficult early years. (For a sense of how far they've come, consider that their early performances were sometimes singled out and cut from Korean TV broadcasts. Or that they recorded their first studio album in a garage. Or that, for a time, other K-pop fandoms systematically attacked BTS's reputation by spreading false rumors.) The Hot 100 No. 1

A

distinction is a point of pride for BTS's dedicated and highly organized fans, known as ARMY, who helped get them there. But like many of the records that BTS sets in America, the achievement is also a reminder of how hard it is for even massively popular artists who don't perform in English to make inroads in the US music industry.

When BTS first announced "Dynamite," they emphasized that it wasn't a permanent pivot from singing in Korean. The seven members—RM, Jin, Suga, J-Hope, Jimin, V, and Jungkook—came across the track while working on their upcoming album and decided to release it as a single with the original English lyrics. The euphoric, late-summer bop was meant to soothe listeners around the world who had been having a hard year because of the COVID-19 pandemic. When "Dynamite" dropped a week and a half ago, it shattered streaming records. American music critics immediately remarked on its catchiness and broadly appealing retro sound. The video—a sun-drenched, SoCal-inspired tribute to all things '70s—had the biggest YouTube premiere for a music video ever, with 101.1 million views in 24 hours.

These weren't unusual milestones for BTS, who had gained even more fans since the pandemic began. What was unusual was that American radio stations started to spin "Dynamite," giving it the sort of play that had been denied to previous Korean-language hit singles, like "Boy With Luv" and "ON." US radio generally doesn't play much non-English pop, and because radio play is one of the metrics used to calculate the Hot 100 (along with streaming and sales), artists who don't perform in English have a harder time making it to No. 1. (The same goes for Latin pop, too, though the success of Luis Fonsi's "Despacito" in 2017 has been credited with helping to open up the chart for Spanish music.) "Dynamite" is radiant, feel-good pop, but the fact that it was in English helped it to reach new heights.

The industry's aversion to non-English-language music extends from the charts to highly visible spaces such as the Grammys and the VMAs—shows that even have long histories of overlooking some English-speaking artists, particularly Black artists. These platforms effectively marginalize different groups, as Marian Liu wrote for *The Washington Post*, by filtering certain musicians into other, implicitly less prestigious categories, including "Best Progressive R&B," "Best K-Pop," and "Best Rap Album." BTS has nonetheless managed to enter these fraught spaces, in some cases peripherally, and only after years of proving their commercial value and ability to draw an audience.

A

When I wrote about becoming a fan of BTS last year, I spoke with the South Korean critic Kim Young-dae about the xenophobia that the band has faced in the US over the course of their rise. (Earlier this year, a *Howard Stern Show* staffer joked about the group having the coronavirus, and fans recently circulated a clip of a radio-station host mocking BTS's Korean lyrics on air.) Because the American music industry is hesitant to call Asian artists "pop stars," Kim said, ARMY was essential in fighting this institutional conservatism. By aggressively streaming, buying, and sharing BTS's music, these fans forced a dinosaur-like industry to pay attention.

These strategies and the grassroots initiatives have been collectively developed and tested by ARMY over the years. In her book *BTS and ARMY Culture*, the South Korean film-studies scholar Jeeheng Lee devotes a full chapter to ARMY's herculean promotional efforts on behalf of the band. One example she mentions comes from 2018, during which fans outlined seven goals to achieve for BTS: a Top 10 entry on the *Billboard* Hot 100; a No. 1 album on the *Billboard* 200; Gold and Platinum Recording Industry Association of America certifications; nominations for the AMAs and the Grammy Awards; and 29 consecutive weeks at

No. 1 on the *Billboard* Social 50 chart. Fan accounts on Twitter and other platforms posted progress updates on metrics such as album purchases and radio-audience impressions. ARMYs educated one another about intricate charting rules and country-specific criteria, and reminded people to stream BTS's music regularly and correctly (that is, avoiding bot-like behavior such as looping). Other fans took it upon themselves to call their local radio stations weekly and request BTS songs. By the end of the year, ARMY had achieved all seven goals. Many of these strategies remain widely used today and were crucial to the success of "Dynamite."

OVER THE YEARS, US interviewers have asked BTS if they would ever switch to making music in English, only to get the same answer: *No*. For the seven members, performing in Korean is essential to their identity as a group. Though BTS is known for complex choreography, impeccable live vocals, and energetic concerts, their lyrics matter too. The group has made albums that critique aspects of Korean culture and society, including mental-health stigmas and the rigid school system. Its rappers often write intricate wordplay into their rhymes. One of my favorite early tracks is "Paldogangsan," whose lyrics are largely written in regional dialect, or *satoori*, highlighting how many different, geographically specific ways there are of speaking Korean throughout the peninsula. When BTS performed at the Grammys for the first time earlier this year, accompanying Lil Nas X for an "Old Town Road" medley, RM's lines played with the homophones "homie" in English and "호미 (*homi*)" in Korean, which refers to a farming tool. His short verse effectively nodded to both the rap and country influences of the original song.

BTS fans around the world regularly look up lyric translations, contrary to what some American music critics believe, and many learn Korean to better appreciate the group's work. In her book, Lee spends another full chapter on how fans overcome language barriers. In particular, she describes the linguistic and cultural reversal that takes place between Korean speakers and English speakers when it comes to BTS's music. As a community, ARMY relies heavily on fans who translate songs, videos, interviews, and social media posts into other languages for their fellow fans. The work of Korean-to-English translators in particular is difficult, unpaid, and time-consuming—if highly respected. "The attitude of Western fans, who waive their prestige within the world order and readily embrace minor cultures is to me like a breeze of fresh air," Lee writes of this "reversal" she has witnessed. I myself have taken

Korean-language classes to supplement the organic independent learning I was already doing to understand BTS's work. I also have friends of Korean descent who, after getting into BTS, began learning or improving their Korean partly as a way of connecting with their heritage.

So, for some fans, the ascendancy of "Dynamite" is bound to be bittersweet. Whether BTS intended to or not, the only English-language single they've released in seven years has become their biggest chart success yet, outperforming the dozens of more artistically ambitious records that they wrote or produced in Korean. "We don't want to change our identity or our genuineness to get the No. 1," RM, the group's leader, told *Entertainment Weekly* in 2019. "Like if we sing suddenly in full English, and change all these other things, then that's not BTS. We'll do everything, we'll try. But if we couldn't get No. 1 or No. 5, that's okay."

If anyone can get a Korean song to No. 1 on the Hot 100, it's the group that reached No. 4 with a Korean song earlier this year—that same track, "ON," won BTS three VMAs last weekend. They don't need to alter their DNA. "Dynamite" is likely to reach even more listeners who don't think language differences are a reason to ignore good music, listeners who might keep an eye out for a new album or dive into BTS's deep Korean

A

discography. The Talking Heads frontman David Byrne declared in a 1999 *New York Times* piece: "To restrict your listening to English-language pop is like deciding to eat the same meal for the rest of your life." ARMY couldn't agree more.

BTS'S "LIFE GOES ON" DID THE IMPOSSIBLE

November 2020

MAYBE IT'S BECAUSE THE PANDEMIC has warped my sense of time, but it feels like just yesterday that BTS got their first No. 1 song on the *Billboard* Hot 100. The South Korean pop group's first all-English single, "Dynamite," was everywhere—in commercials, at the MTV Video Music Awards, on the radio. In September, the song made them the first all–South Korean group to top the chart. Just last week, it landed BTS a Grammy nomination—the first such nod for a Korean group. (These guys break records so often that reciting their achievements can sometimes feel exhausting.)

When I wrote in September that BTS would one day get a No. 1 hit with a song in their native Korean, I didn't think it'd happen less than three months later. Today, the band topped the Hot 100 again, this time with "Life Goes On," a hip-hop–inflected, guitar-laced single about the struggles of pandemic life. Unlike "Dynamite," "Life Goes On" received minimal promotion and radio play, which makes its debut at No. 1 that much more unbelievable. Enormous physical and digital sales—led by the group's dedicated fans, ARMY—pushed the single to the top. In other words, "Life Goes On" is currently the biggest song on the charts, released by the biggest musical group in the world, and there's a good chance you haven't heard it.

The lackluster radio spins for "Life Goes On" aren't surprising; many non-English-language artists struggle to break into the mainstream. Even Latin music continues to be siloed, despite its enormous popularity, its artistic innovation, and the fact that Spanish is the second-most-spoken language in the United States. The takeaway seems clear: If you don't primarily perform in English, you need to outsell your closest competitors many times over—or secure a radio-friendly collaboration or remix—to have a shot at reaching No. 1 on the Hot 100. The success of "Life Goes On," the lead single from BTS's highly anticipated new record, *Be* (on which every member has writing credits), goes some way toward proving the extent of their star power.

Be provides ample evidence as well. The album is a kind of musical document of the members' thoughts and feelings about losing a year to the pandemic. Unable to embark on their world stadium tour, BTS turned their attention back to making music, taking

A

on a greater role in songwriting, producing, and even directing. The result: a carefully composed eight-track album of intimate and stylistically diverse songs in Korean, capped by the juggernaut "Dynamite." Yesterday, the record debuted at No. 1 on the *Billboard* Hot 200.

If you're familiar with BTS's music, "Life Goes On" is both a perfect and unlikely candidate for their biggest Korean song yet. In an interview, the group's leader, RM, described the track as "really calm, almost contemplative," adding, "It might even come off as bland next to 'Dynamite.'" Unlike many of BTS's hit singles, the song has no compulsively danceable beat, no maximalist production, and no intricate choreography. But its gentle, stripped-down melody is memorable, like a tune you've heard somewhere before. "Life Goes On" aches with longing for a different time, for human connection. This emotional register—nostalgic, vulnerable, melancholy yet optimistic—pervades BTS's work and captures the core of their appeal. That tone is most apparent in 2017's "Spring Day," arguably the group's best song and one that holds particular meaning for South Korean listeners, given that many interpreted it as a tribute to the young victims of the Sewol ferry disaster. But nearly every BTS song seeks, in some way, to assure the listener: *You are not alone.*

"Life Goes On" attempts to commiserate without getting consumed by grief. "One day, the world stopped / Without any prior warning," Jungkook sings in a voice edged with exhaustion. "On a street with footsteps since erased, / Here I am, fallen on the ground," Jimin continues, rising to a falsetto. In his rap verse, RM paints an image of trying to outrun a rain cloud before admitting his helplessness: "I must merely be human." The members each add their own texture to the song, creating a sense of togetherness out of individual alienation. "Here, hold my hand / Let's fly to that future," Jungkook and Jin sing together before the chorus erupts: "Like an echo in a forest / The day will surely return / As if nothing happened / *Yeah life goes on . . . like this again.*"

If "Life Goes On" received airplay, non-Korean-speaking audiences would, of course, not understand most of the lyrics. But the aural warmth of the vocal harmonies, combined with the English refrains ("Life goes on" and "I remember"), make it the sort of healing track that could resonate with many listeners in a difficult year. (Alicia Keys seemed to agree, posting a short, all-English cover of the song over Thanksgiving weekend that went viral.)

The other new songs on *Be* create a more holistic emotional picture of pandemic life; the album is like a

A

giant mood ring orbiting the listener. "Fly to My Room" is a jaunty track, full of delicious synth stabs and playful electric organ, about finding adventure amid claustrophobia. ("This year's been stolen from me / I'm still in bed / I feel nauseous / *It's killin' me slowly,*" Jimin sings.) The midnight-colored lullaby "Blue & Grey," originally written by V for his solo mixtape, reflects on the depression and malaise of quarantine existence. ("As ever, is this blue question mark / unease or gloom? / Perhaps we really are animals of regret, / or I've been born by loneliness," Suga raps.) These songs couldn't be more different in energy or tone; back to back, they speak to BTS's stylistic omnivorousness.

Be might be fueled by frustration and powerlessness, but it seeks to energize, not wallow. "Telepathy," a funky bop, delights in the thrill of a long-awaited reunion ("I think about these streets of ours that the star has allowed for us," RM raps). Perhaps my favorite song on the album is "Dis-ease." Largely written by J-Hope, it's about the sickness of overworking; an old-school hip-hop track with a slick, half-time bridge written by Jimin, this is for rap lovers ("It feels as though I should be doing something to the point my body shatters / but I'm just a bastard who eats all three meals a day," J-Hope snarls). Aside from "Skit" (a recording of the members celebrating the No. 1 win of

"Dynamite"), the final new song is "Stay," a dance track originally intended for Jungkook's solo mixtape that seems designed for the catharsis of a stadium performance. Jin sings his own lyrics ("When I open my eyes, it's again / A room devoid of people") in a near whisper before the track builds to a pulsating beat for its anthem-like chorus: *Yeah, I know you always stay.* Those words hold particular meaning for ARMY, especially those who organize to stream and buy BTS's music in defiance of an indifferent industry.

When I said that BTS breaks records so often that reciting them can feel exhausting, I didn't mean to suggest that those victories have become less meaningful over time, or that the group's enormous success somehow dilutes its discrete achievements. But these records, no matter how dutifully listed, do not capture what is most interesting about BTS, which is their ability to be perfectly understood by fans around the world who themselves don't speak a word of Korean.

Fortunately, that cultural identity remains essential to the group's artistic identity. In a recent interview, RM referenced the famed Korean abstract artist Whanki Kim to make a point: "After moving to New York [in the '60s], he embraced the style of artists like Mark Rothko and Adolph Gottlieb, but then [Kim] said, 'I'm Korean, and I can't do anything not Korean.

I can't do anything apart from this, because I am an outsider.'" The same, RM said, applies to himself, but it can also describe BTS. The language they speak, their steady sense of self, is a strength. Once pushed to the margins, these "outsiders" decided to create their own world and welcome everyone in.

THE ASTONISHING
DUALITY OF BTS

———

December 2020

BTS HAS SPENT ENOUGH TIME in the pop-music strato-
sphere that it can be easy to forget, or surprising to
learn, about the years they spent at the basement level.
Back in 2014, for the first anniversary of their debut,
the group's seven members celebrated by cleaning the
tiny dorm they shared and cooking a nice meal. They
recorded a video of themselves for fans, soaking seaweed
for a traditional Korean birthday soup, blowing up
smiley-face balloons, vacuuming the living room, and
decorating a cake. Their then-19-year-old leader, RM,
attempts to peel an onion. "Man, I wonder how my
mother did this every day," he says, sounding embar-
rassed. "The members always tell me not to drive or
cook for the sake of world peace."

Unbothered by the cramped quarters, they all seem
giddy about reaching a career milestone together, even
though they are very much still at the start of their journey. Watching this video now—six years, seven studio
albums, and a mountain of broken industry records

later—isn't just an exercise in nostalgia for the early days of RM, Jin, Suga, J-Hope, Jimin, V, and Jungkook. It's a reminder of how the world's biggest band became so popular in the first place, an object lesson in making the most of what little you have.

Humility was useful in 2020, a year that brought the entertainment industry, as well as the world, to its knees. The coronavirus pandemic led to canceled tours and closed venues; when musicians performed, they did so from home or to empty seats. This new reality could've hurt BTS, an act known for putting on spectacular, high-energy live concerts. (Last year, they sold out a show at London's Wembley Stadium in 90 minutes.) Used to thriving on elaborately designed stages before tens of thousands of people, they suddenly found themselves recording TV appearances from their practice space and executing grandiose comeback routines with only staffers cheering them on. But although BTS is no longer a ragtag rookie group, their modest beginnings prepared them to succeed during a year that would have had them shrink their ambitions.

Originally, 2020 promised a world tour for *Map of the Soul: 7,* the group's most sophisticated album to date and one that fans had hoped would land the pop stars their first Grammy nomination. The 20-track record feels like a mature artistic statement—the sole exception

A

being a forgettable remix featuring Sia—in which each song has a distinct style and philosophical perspective on the nature of fame, connection, and creation. Good luck pinning down the album's sound; the genres distort beautifully, like an oil slick, whether on the full-group efforts or on the solo tracks, each of which presents a different aspect of the members' persona. Sample hypnotic Latin guitars on Jimin's "Filter," wistful R&B on Jungkook's "My Time," dreamy jangle pop on Jin's "Moon," and nostalgic arena rock on V's "Inner Child." Muse over the Jungian reflections woven into the cerebral rap-rock of RM's "Intro: Persona," the visceral emo hip-hop of Suga's "Interlude: Shadow," and the exuberant Afrobeat rhythms of J-Hope's "Outro: Ego." Lyrically, the album tells the story of a group that has pondered the most intimate and extraordinary aspects of superstardom. The standout track, "Black Swan," layers dark trap beats and traditional Asian strings over verses about how artists losing their love for their art is like dying—a fittingly profound theme for an album they never got the chance to perform live in 2020.

"We've struggled this year," Jin told me in an email interview with the group. "Most of the plans that we arranged two years ago have vanished, but in the midst of this, we worked hard and . . . did something meaningful." For BTS, *something meaningful* is getting nominated for a Grammy months after performing at the Grammys—and being the first Korean group to do either. They released their fifth *Billboard* Hot 200–topping album in a row with *BE*. They landed three No. 1 songs on the Hot 100, including their first English-language single, "Dynamite," and their dark-horse hit, "Life Goes On." Although "Dynamite" is BTS's biggest song thus far, RM said the latter achievement made him feel "double the joy because, as you said, it was a Korean song. It's a title given to us by our fans," referring to the fact that, "Life Goes On" received virtually no radio play, so purchases and streams by ARMY pushed it to the top of the chart, making it the first Korean song to get there.

The hyperbolic language that surrounds BTS today (*global phenomenon! K-pop sensation! First Korean act to . . . !*) can distract from the fact that the group doesn't need big stadiums or epic set lists to reach audiences. They're comfortable talking to fans via impromptu live-streams in their PJs and posting acoustic song covers on Twitter. And unlike many idol groups, the members of BTS have always addressed the subject of mental health in their lyrics and in their lives. That candor resonated this year in particular, as they've spoken about feeling angry, helpless, and depressed.

A

For his birthday earlier this month, Jin released a solo track called "Abyss," along with a note explaining that he wrote it after experiencing severe burnout and seeking counseling for anxious thoughts. When I asked whether he found this honesty difficult, he demurred. "I don't know if it was hard to share this," Jin said. "I think music is just another form of expression. If I hadn't written the text on the blog, I think people might have only guessed I was in such a state." Moved by his words and the song's delicate beauty, some fans shared their own struggles on social media. "If you know how to deal with your mental health, it's fine to keep it to yourself," Jin said. "But if you don't, I think it's good you open up because you might have someone around you who knows how to handle it."

This week brought a duo of surprise SoundCloud releases also intended to comfort: Jimin's "Christmas Love" and V's "Snow Flower." Jimin, to accompany his bright, nostalgic track, wrote a message about feeling joy despite the social scripts of adulthood: "Instead of dismissing your feelings as 'cringey' or 'childish,' as we often do, I hope the day will come that we can all happily enjoy these emotions together." In his note for the sweetly jazzy "Snow Flower," V wrote, "This year felt like time stopped, and I think there will be many people who feel more anxiety and depression as the end of the year approaches. For at least today, I hope the white flowers come down to your hearts and you feel even just a little bit of warm comfort and happiness."

AGAINST THIS BACKDROP OF vulnerability, BTS also offered audiences solace through eye-catching stages. With their tour postponed indefinitely, they reconfigured their songs for online consumption. A cozy summer performance, and a two-day fall concert attended by nearly 1 million people, tested the boundaries of virtual live shows. "I don't think our music or performance has been limited, but it's just the way we deliver the best performance that has changed," V said of the group's pandemic-era work. In 2019, one of BTS's best performances was a 37-minute set for South Korea's Melon Music Awards, featuring live horses, seven solo stages, a lung-busting dance break, and a sea of extras. In 2020, many of their best performances were much smaller but the bar remained high. For *The Late Late Show With James Corden*, they sang "Life Goes On" while walking (thanks to editing trickery) through the same room over and over again, conveying the claustrophobia of quarantine life.

When BTS returned to the Melon Music Awards this year, they wowed not with scale, but with precise choreography. Jimin and Jungkook performed an exquisite and technically difficult *pas de deux* during the song "Black Swan." And the group unveiled an endlessly rewatchable Michael Jackson–esque dance break for "Dynamite." "To be honest, I think that performance was close to perfection," J-Hope told me. That means a lot coming from the group's famously meticulous dance leader. "It wasn't something that could be done by myself, but everything was in sync—the costumes, lights, choreography, camerawork, and the [other] members."

Sometimes, putting on the "best performance" meant no dancing at all. For their NPR Tiny Desk Concert in September, BTS did the whole set (mostly) sitting down on stools, befitting the institution's more laid-back vibe. And "Life Goes On" is their first title track to not have official choreography. "We think the song's emotion goes better without any choreo," Suga said of the understated single, which feels as though it was written not from idols to fans, but from one human to another. The rest of *BE* comes across that way too—raw and personal, like a mixtape designed for your closest friends. In his "Life Goes On" verse, Suga references a gorgeously introspective song from his latest solo mixtape called "People," whose lyrics are similarly about taking an optimistic view of life's vagaries. "The message of 'People' was something like 'so what, life still goes on,' so I wanted to extend that message," Suga said.

At the end of 2020, as vaccine distribution begins, the notion that *life goes on* might sound more plausible than it once did. For BTS, as for everyone else, next year looks blurry, but it at least has a clear starting point. "2021 begins with the Grammys," J-Hope said. "They say that the first step [of the year] is important, so I hope we have good results there." BTS is nominated for Best Pop Duo/Group Performance for "Dynamite" and are expected to perform, although many fans were disappointed that *Map of the Soul: 7* wasn't recognized. "It would be such an honor to earn a nod for our album some day," the group said.

BTS hopes that the rest of 2021 will bring with it the possibility of live concerts. "I want to show our fans our 'On' performance," Jungkook said of their most extravagantly choreographed song. "If fans want to see 'Louder Than Bombs,' of course we can perform" it too, he added of a fan-favorite song that I asked about. The year ahead might yield more solo work, including highly anticipated projects from V and Jungkook. "This year has been packed so I couldn't find that much time to work on it. I will try to perfect it next year," V said of his mixtape. "When I revisit the songs I made, I am not fully satisfied. So I honestly don't know just yet!"

Jungkook said of his record's release, though he has written or produced multiple songs this year, including the dreamy ballad "Still With You."

Whatever happens at the Grammys, the nomination of "Dynamite" is a huge deal. As Jimin put it in a recent *Vanity Fair* interview, "Worldwide, when people look at us, they might not know what country we're from. They might not know what little rural town us bumpkins came from. And yet, there we are on the highest stage, in the running to win an award." That symbolism of the Grammys stage, the legitimacy it confers, is real. But BTS's humble past is ever present. They seem, at all times, to remember where they came from, even as they seek to not be confined by the label of *K-pop*. "Producer Bang [Si-hyuk] once told me that I was 'local,' and I think that's something that describes me accurately," RM told me, referring to the founder of BTS's label, Big Hit Entertainment. "I am also aware that, as millennials, limiting ourselves to a certain region is not desirable." With BTS, the only constant is their duality—they're "local" yet global, industry outsiders on the inside, equally skilled at intimacy and pageantry.

This year might have looked very different for BTS if their bond hadn't been forged in the crucible of those early years. "When life gets tough or it's hard to find motivation in life, what keeps me going are the relationships and the energy I get from them—our members, the people around me and our fans are all so valuable," Jimin told me. His sentiment is illustrated in the *BE* track, "Skit," which documents the group's reaction to learning of their first Hot 100 No. 1. The members yell and joke about skipping dance practice to grab a drink. The track ends with RM asking J-Hope, "Hope-ah, don't you think this is what happiness is like?"

Six years ago, BTS gathered for a quieter sort of celebration. At the end of their first-anniversary video, they sit on their dorm-room floor around a table piled with delicious food, laughing. They sing "Happy Birthday" to themselves. Then, together, they begin to eat. It looks like happiness too.

THE SPECTACULAR
VINDICATION OF BTS

───────

December 2021

FOR 20 MONTHS, I WAS haunted by two fears: that some things would last forever, and that others would be lost forever. I imagined a world in which the norms of the pandemic—masks, rapid tests, postponed weddings, canceled family gatherings, lost jobs, prohibitive travel restrictions—became permanent. I tried to accept the death of certain dreams and plans in the face of a starker reality. A virus had killed millions. I, like many people, had lost loved ones. Time warped around me, as it did for so many people. Some days, it moved like molasses. On others, like the all-too-rare moments when I saw family and friends, it seemed to flow like a river that I couldn't stop or outrun.

Then, for two weeks at the end of 2021, I tried to control time for myself.

In September, as live music was returning in earnest, BTS announced their first in-person concerts in two years. They'd play four nights at the open-air SoFi

Stadium, in Los Angeles, where the Super Bowl would be held in 2022. (Mask wearing and proof of vaccination or a recent negative COVID-19 test would be required for all attendees.) Knowing that demand was bound to be fierce, I hoped to attend just once, trying to ignore the fact that I had secured tickets to five different shows in three different cities for BTS's planned 2020 tour in support of their album *Map of the Soul: 7*.

In early February 2020, before the coronavirus had shut down life in the United States, I coordinated with ARMY friends in different states to use our coveted pre-sale codes and obtain the best possible seats. Even before BTS released its English-language singles and multiplied the size of its fanbase, ticketing for concerts was commonly referred to by ARMYs as a "bloodbath," for the demand that outpaced supply by orders of magnitude. As the reality of the pandemic set in, the "Map of the Soul" shows were postponed, then later canceled altogether. I would have to start from scratch to get tickets, only this time I'd be competing with millions of new fans who had discovered BTS in the preceding year and a half—for just four concerts. Thanks to a lot of planning, stress, and luck, I managed to get tickets to all four dates. For one week, I'd share hotel rooms with close friends, attend every show, visit fan-organized pop-ups, wear clothes other than sweatpants or leggings, and blast BTS while carpooling in LA traffic. And for the first time in months, I smiled at the idea of time standing still.

By all appearances, time had been kind to the seven members of BTS. Already global superstars before the pandemic, RM, Jin, Suga, J-Hope, Jimin, V, and Jungkook had only gotten bigger since 2020. They'd released three albums and scored six *Billboard* Hot 100 No. 1 songs, in both English and Korean. They won millions of new fans and became the first K-pop act to receive a Grammy nomination last year for their single "Dynamite" (followed by another nomination this year for "Butter"). This fall, they spoke at the United Nations General Assembly for the third time, accompanying South Korean President Moon Jae-in as special envoys. So when the group finally took the stage in Los Angeles in late November and early December 2021, the shows might have seemed like a simple victory lap. In truth, they also served as a kind of vindication of BTS—of their talent, authenticity, reach, and emotional connection with fans. All of those things had been called into question by critics, or at times by the artists themselves, in 2021. The four nights were loud, ecstatic, and poignant proof that they had all been wrong.

BTS SHOWS ARE REMARKABLE affairs, known for elaborate production design, pairing demanding choreography with live vocals, goofy banter, sincere speeches, inside jokes, and a high level of crowd participation by their fans, known as ARMY. I had experienced all of this as a brand-new (and somewhat intimidated) ARMY attending my first BTS concert in May 2019, but I still felt unprepared for the LA shows, which were named for the band's latest single, "Permission to Dance." In the preceding weeks, I couldn't conceive of spectacles of sound, movement, and community after spending much of the past two years in silence, stillness, and solitude.

Imagine some 50,000 people gathered in the darkness as lights blink around them like stars. They're dancing like one body, singing with a single voice in a language that may not be their own. Many of the people in this little universe understand how easily their happiness at seeing a "boy band" or a "K-pop sensation" could be derided as trivial or childish. But that condescension has no place here. As the night goes on, thoughts of what they've suffered or lost recently grow dimmer, and the strangers around them start to look like family.

A

This is the spell that a BTS concert can cast. When the group opened the first show in LA with their inaugural in-person performance of the adrenaline-pumping "ON," the air crackled. When the beginning notes of the moody gem "Black Swan" started, the stadium seemed to hold its breath. The group members staged a gorgeously choreographed sequence, alongside white-feathered dancers, that seemed to belong in a baroque theater rather than a pop concert. The back-to-back, live-band renditions of their smash singles "Dynamite" and "Butter" were like aural serotonin, particularly on day two, when an effervescent Megan Thee Stallion strutted out to rap her verse in the "Butter" remix.

Watching these two performances in particular, I thought of the critics who had accused BTS of abandoning their identity as Korean artists—all for releasing three songs in English. As the show continued, I watched BTS perform Korean tracks from their largely self-written 2020 record *BE*, including their Hot 100 No. 1 single "Life Goes On." The set list reaffirmed the group's roots, featuring many of the Korean-language tracks ("DNA," "Blood Sweat & Tears," "I Need U," "Idol") that had helped them break out. And when BTS paused between songs, many members abandoned the English remarks they had practiced and instead shared their feelings in their native tongue, as an interpreter translated their words for the stadium. The shows, especially coming weeks after the group's official appearances as cultural ambassadors for South Korea, seemed to obviate lingering questions about their authenticity.

Alongside complaints about their supposedly waning Koreanness, BTS have faced renewed criticism about how popular they really are. Some American critics have a tendency to admit to the group's enormous appeal while also trying to undercut it. "If you look at the charts . . . you're going to get a completely distorted idea of how popular BTS actually are," argued a *Stereogum* piece that accused ARMYs in particular of "gaming the system" for organizing streaming and buying campaigns to support the group's music, thus destroying the legitimacy of the *Billboard* charts. The piece also lamented the death of "organic popularity" in pop music, even though BTS came from an upstart record label and slowly earned a following through social media and word of mouth. ARMYs, who were used to such selective and simplistic accusations, took to social media to criticize and rebut the story's claims, but even non-fans and other music journalists expressed their bewilderment at the article and its apparently ahistorical view of fan engagement. One article commenter noted that, well before BTS existed, during the height of the physical-CD era, fans would regularly bulk purchase copies of an artist's latest release to show their support. Others raised their eyebrows at the notion that the *Billboard* charts ever had a reputation as reliable and objective indicators of popularity.

A June cover story by *Billboard* questioned whether BTS's grassroots fan efforts were being secretly coordinated by their own label; BTS and their record label's parent company, Hybe, denied this specious suggestion. "It just feels like we're easy targets because we're a boy band, a K-pop act, and we have this high fan loyalty," the leader, RM, said at the time, summarizing the feelings of many ARMYs who have long believed they've been unfairly singled out, despite working to abide by arcane and ever-changing chart rules.

In press interviews ahead of the SoFi shows, RM took further aim at attempts to shade BTS's success and fans, subtly mocking the notion that ARMYs were bots or just 15-year-old girls. In recent years, BTS has been quick to not only defend their fans, but also make clear that they don't see ARMY as a homogenous, single-minded entity. As E. Alex Jung wrote in a 2018 *Vulture* piece, "BTS innately understand that they owe their success to their fans, and that theirs is the result of a tight symbiosis . . . This isn't a group that thinks it's bigger than its fans." As any casual observer of the dynamics between pop musicians and their fans can attest, this sense of mutual respect isn't guaranteed. Sometimes, artists' appreciation for their fans can seem obligatory or superficial. Not so with BTS. In a video recorded ahead of the group's first speech before the UN General Assembly in 2018, Suga talked about how fans of idol groups are often unfairly belittled for their dedication, when in fact such loyalty doesn't come easily. "It's not easy to do such things just because you like someone," he said. This might seem like a simple statement, but it readily acknowledges the difference between appreciating an artist versus taking concrete action to champion them out in the world. "When we're talking about the pop-music industry, authenticity isn't always literally about who you are or what you are thinking," Kim Youngdae told me back in 2019. "But it's about how you convinced the audience that this is about them. That this is about us. Authenticity is more about relationships." That relationship is one that BTS and ARMY have actively cultivated and nurtured since 2013; even fans who came to the group in 2021 can consider themselves part of this longer lineage.

Because BTS's following had grown so dramatically since the start of the pandemic, I was looking forward to attending a show filled with newcomers and veterans

A

alike. At the stadium, my heart swelled at the sheer diversity of the attendees: older women with purple highlights and tattoos, couples wearing matching BTS headbands, young people conversing excitedly in French or Japanese or Arabic, middle-aged men in T-shirts emblazoned with JUNGKOOK or JIMIN, friends carrying Pride flags, and families of multiple generations hauling bags of merch.

I spent an entire day with a teenage girl, her mother, and her aunt after a friend connected us—the trio had an extra floor-seat ticket that came with access to that day's soundcheck rehearsal. Pure gold, in other words. (I'm hardly kidding: Scalpers had been trying to sell these tickets for $30,000.) When I met my three concert buddies for the first time outside SoFi, we hugged as though we had known each other our entire lives; such was the natural sense of camaraderie I had come to expect after dozens of chance encounters with fans in the wild over the years. By then I'd become familiar with ARMY's gifting culture, which can involve preparing and distributing goodie bags, original fanart, jewelry, snacks, handmade stickers, and signs. As a newbie attending my first BTS concert in 2019, I had been only a recipient of these freebies. But for the SoFi shows, I came prepared with purple sachets filled with photocards, candy, earplugs (for hearing safety), and cough drops (in anticipation of all the singing and screaming). When I handed them out ahead of the show, it felt like an ARMY rite of passage.

While standing in the hours-long lines to get into the stadium, people amused themselves by playing BTS songs on their phones and dancing to BTS routines. I recognized some of the choreography I saw other ARMYs doing, and my body involuntarily mirrored their movements in miniature. I am a terrible dancer, and yet for BTS songs, the muscle memory was instinctive.

I overheard some attendees telling new acquaintances the story of how they had gotten into the group's music—through a friend, a child, a YouTube link from a coworker, a late-night TV performance caught by chance. All of this looked like organic fandom to me.

THE IMPERMANENCE OF BEAUTY, the beauty of impermanence—these are things BTS understand well. Their lyrics overflow with self-aware references to the ephemerality of both fame and contentment. Take the 2016 song "Epilogue: Young Forever": "This can't be mine forever, the loud applause . . . Though there's no eternal audience, I'm going to sing." At a press conference with BTS the day after their first concert, I had a

A

chance to ask the members how their opening show at SoFi compared with their performances at the American Music Awards a week earlier, where they picked up three awards including Artist of the Year. Through a translator, Jungkook spoke of how the cheers from ARMYs who attended the AMAs had given them energy that they then carried into the concerts. It was as though the pandemic, with its lack of in-person performances, had given them a scarcity mindset when it came to hearing their fans' voices in real life. I asked this question in part because I had been one of those fans at the AMAs, which were also held in Los Angeles. The awards crucially marked BTS's first performance in front of a live audience since before the pandemic.

During the press conference, I thought back to the last time I had seen BTS: on a freezing-cold Manhattan morning in February 2020, at a *Today Show* appearance where they were promoting their new album, *Map of the Soul: 7*. When the record dropped hours earlier, I listened to it in the exhausted-yet-wide-awake sort of haze I'd come to associate with BTS releases, which are usually scheduled according to Korean time. The short interview they gave outside on the *Today Show* Plaza, before a crowd of fans who had camped overnight in the cold for the chance to see them, exuded an enthusiasm for the future that was promptly punished as the pandemic began to shut down daily life across the globe.

That memory floated to the surface of my mind when I showed up to the Microsoft Theater on a hot afternoon in late November. Before even entering the building, I knew I was in the right place. Plenty of popular and well-loved artists were also performing that day, but the crowd was overwhelmingly composed of ARMY, as indicated by the purple face masks, headbands, bag charms, and BTS-themed outfit choices. Inside the theater, before the show started, the audience started doing coordinated fan chants (essentially shouting out the members' names in an official order) and cheering "BTS! BTS! BTS!" any time things got too quiet. As I expected, ARMY had turned the American Music Awards into a mini BTS concert. During the group's two stage appearances, a collaboration with Coldplay called "My Universe" and a solo performance of their smash hit "Butter," the roars vibrated the air. Every fan in attendance seemed to understand their role that day: to reassure BTS, by sheer force of sound and presence, that they hadn't gone anywhere. And the group responded by reminding ARMYs, if they had ever forgotten, that live BTS concerts are considered legendary for a reason.

A

That same energy radiated from each member under the hot lights of SoFi Stadium a week later: RM's fierce and authoritative presence, Jin's bottomless vocal virtuosity, Suga's effortlessly charismatic cool, J-Hope's peerless dance mastery, Jimin's intoxicating command of movement, V's singular vocals and aura, and Jungkook's tireless domination of the stage. When they moved together, you could not look away.

Still, on the last night of the stadium shows, BTS offered a window into the looming sense of expiration they feel. During the final speeches, an emotional V said in Korean that they "had doubts if there would be any ARMYs left" after two years. Through tears, RM said in English that he spent much of the pandemic being afraid of their future, wondering, "What if I got too old to do this, to dance like I was 23 or 25, when we were so new and fresh?" He talked about working out for the past two years just to prepare for these four concerts, and admitted that though they had no idea when they could perform again, he was now less scared. "I promise that . . . I'll be even better when I'm 30, or 35, or 40," he said.

By the end of it all, I had arrived at a similar realization. None of us could stop time, but we didn't need to. I'd always have my memories of the Los Angeles shows:

Eating bags of too-salty chips for dinner in a hotel room. Practicing fan chants for different songs in pajamas and getting tounge-tied over the same tricky lines again and again. Getting an impromptu commemorative tattoo in a new pal's living room, because why not? Eating ice cream with dear friends whom I first met online back in that terrible month of March 2020—friends who are living proof that Twitter isn't completely awful, proof of how BTS has brought love into my life in ways I couldn't have predicted. Dancing in the stadium with an ecstatic, beer-sipping seatmate who had flown from Texas by herself, knowing that when she arrived at the concert she wouldn't truly be alone. Seeing some of my favorite songs performed live, alongside people who loved them, too, but in their own completely singular way.

The concerts that BTS delivered, and the community with whom I shared those experiences, made me less afraid of holding these moments of joy gently, and then letting them go. They reminded me that the future would bring joy again. That night, BTS sang the fan favorite "Home," whose lyrics are about feeling brave enough to go out into the world, because you know you have somewhere, and someone, safe to return to. After the shows ended, I learned that BTS grossed $33.3 million and sold more than 200,000 tickets; their SoFi run is one of the best-selling concert runs at

A

a single venue in history. But those numbers don't capture everything. The image that stays with me is of people's hands reaching up in unison, through the fluttering confetti, toward the sky. Eyes wide, as if in disbelief. As if nobody had told them that going to a concert could feel like coming home.

BTS GETS IT

June 2022

THE WHITE HOUSE BRIEFING ROOM hadn't been packed like this in ages. That's what journalists kept saying last Tuesday, as more than a hundred of them squeezed into the room, cradling their cameras and murmuring *sorry*s every time they bumped into one another. South Korean media outlets jockeyed for space alongside the usual American networks. A few people joked that the huge crowd was there for Brian Deese, the National Economic Council director, who was also scheduled to speak. Everyone kept checking the time. Then, a few minutes past 2:30 p.m., the blue door at the front of the room slid open and in walked Press Secretary Karine Jean-Pierre, followed by a line of seven young men in immaculate black suits. The camera shutters exploded. BTS had arrived.

Everyone seemed to understand that they were in rare company, even if the gathering's purpose was serious. The biggest band in the world was in the American capital to speak with President Joe Biden about anti-Asian hate crimes and Asian representation. Though their briefing-room appearance lasted fewer than 10 minutes, RM, Jin, Suga, J-Hope, Jimin, V, and Jungkook all took turns speaking, mostly in their native Korean. Through an interpreter, they shared that they'd been devastated by the recent surge in violence against Asian people in the US and spoke about the ability of art to transcend language and culture. "We believe music is always an amazing and wonderful unifier of all things," Jungkook said.

Though some observers might have raised their eyebrows at the visit, the group has a history of addressing social issues through a universal lens—and, of course, bringing visibility to any cause they're associated with. American media coverage of the event seemed to grasp this broader context. Reuters referred to BTS as "a fundraising juggernaut for US social-justice causes," noting the group's donation of $1 million to Black Lives Matter in 2020, which was matched by their fandom, known as ARMY, in a day. Some articles noted the group's three past appearances at the UN General Assembly, and most mentioned how in 2021, after the shooting deaths of eight people in Atlanta, including six Asian women, BTS posted a statement to Twitter in support of #StopAAPI-Hate. In the note, they described instances of racism they had faced before turning their attention outward. "Our own experiences are inconsequential compared to

A

the events that have occurred over the past weeks . . . What is happening right now cannot be dissociated from our identity as Asians." According to Twitter, it was the most retweeted post of 2021.

The question of how to turn heightened awareness into lasting change is a complicated one that many groups—including the Stop AAPI Hate movement—are currently reckoning with. And activists and legal experts have acknowledged the limits of legislation such as the COVID-19 Hate Crimes Act. Where a world-famous band of Korean performers fits in is even more complicated. Last year, I attended a press conference with BTS where another journalist raised the subject. "We in the US had to deal with Asian hate since 2020," she said, going on to ask if the members had any comments "about the positive role that you've taken to help end that Asian hate and show a positive light to Asians and Asian Americans." The question, though well intended, bothered me with its wording. After all, Asian Americans have had to deal with violence and discrimination since long before 2020, and surely *ending hate* against Asian people requires more than just offering them a *positive light*.

Her query seemed to place an unfair burden on the shoulders of seven young musicians who have never claimed to be activists. It was not their responsibility to stop people in America from committing hate crimes, or to inspire would-be attackers to see people of Asian descent as humans deserving of life and safety. But RM replied with grace, saying that as Asians, BTS had felt "the walls" throughout their career—walls that were sometimes visible, sometimes invisible—and that he hoped that their success as artists "can truly help every Asian in the world."

Fast-forward six months to when BTS's visit to the White House was announced and some critics questioned its appropriateness. Why would BTS be asked to talk about issues concerning Asian Americans, who are marginalized in the US in ways that the members, as Koreans in a Korean society, are not? Some suggested that the White House should've instead invited Asian Americans—never mind that the Biden administration had done precisely that two weeks earlier in honor of Asian American, Native Hawaiian, and Pacific Islander Heritage Month. Or that BTS's members have always been careful to acknowledge their perspective as Koreans, not Americans. Or that people who are perceived as Asian in America have been attacked without regard for their citizenship status or what language they speak.

Because of the attention drawn to BTS's meeting with Biden, many AAPI folks ended up projecting their own feelings about Asian identity onto the group. On one hand, some were overjoyed about being represented on a global stage by talented, beloved artists who look like them, or who share their heritage. On the other hand, some voiced their anxiety about the ongoing injustices against their communities that no single speech or tweet can fix. It's true that the ugly illogics of racism are rooted in American history and perpetuated by its institutions. But, to me, that doesn't mean that BTS's trip to the White House, which they paid for themselves, was pointless.

Whatever part BTS plays, plenty of people are embracing the visibility that the band is bringing. "Given their stardom, BTS could easily choose to turn a blind eye and dismiss anti-Asian violence and racism. They choose not to, and neither should anyone else," wrote Jennifer Lee, a professor of social sciences at Columbia University, in a blog post for *Science*. She cited a recent poll that found that at least 15 percent of Asian American adults were victims of hate crimes in 2021, and another report that found that one-third of Americans are still unaware of this rise in violence.

BTS's full, 35-minute conversation with Biden was closed to the press, but an edited video of the meeting was finally uploaded this week by the White House. In it, RM, the group's leader and the only member fluent in English, talks about BTS feeling a "great responsibility" to use their platform to help people. Speaking to Biden in the Oval Office with the other members, RM recalls how the group reacted when they received their invitation to the White House—the disbelief, the excitement. "This is it. Why not? We have to go—we have to go to DC," he remembers them saying. As though their sense of duty kicked in. No, this is not their country, and Biden is not their president. But to do anything less would have gone against who they are.

A

ARTICLE CREDITS

ABOUT THE AUTHOR

LENIKA CRUZ is a senior editor at *The Atlantic*, where she has been a staffer on the culture section since 2014. She has edited stories that have been nominated for James Beard Awards and included in anthologies such as *Best Food Writing*, and one that was named as a Pulitzer Prize finalist. In addition to *The Atlantic*, Lenika's essays, reporting, and criticism have appeared in *LA Weekly*, *Glamour*, *The Rumpus*, *East Bay Express*, and Guam's *Pacific Daily News*. She has spoken about race, culture, and media for the Asian American Journalists Association, the Washington National Cathedral, and Pomona College's Humanities Studio. She has appeared as a guest on NPR's *Code Switch* and *Pop Culture Happy Hour*, *The Atlantic*'s *Review* podcast, *Blank Check*, KPCC, and other radio shows. She is a volunteer contributing editor for the street newspaper *Street Sense*. She graduated from UCLA in 2012 with a BA in English.